HULL TROLLEYBUSES

THE FINAL DECADE

Malcolm Wells and Paul Morfitt

AMBERLEY

First published 2018

Amberley Publishing
The Hill, Stroud
Gloucestershire, GL5 4EP

www.amberley-books.com

ISBN 978 1 4456 8229 7 (print)
ISBN 978 1 4456 8230 3 (ebook)

British Library Cataloguing in Publication Data.
A catalogue record for this book is available from the British Library.

Origination by Amberley Publishing.
Printed in the UK.

Introduction

A promising future for Hull's trolleybuses seemed certain on 2 November 1954 when Sunbeam MF2B trolleybuses Nos 102/3/5 entered service. Their bodies were designed for one-man operation with a front entrance/staircase for boarding and a central exit/staircase for alighting. The design was developed by G. H. Pulfrey (General Manager) and Charles H. Roe. A prototype, No. 101, which entered service in January 1953, received the nickname 'Coronation', which was applied to the production batch. The last, No. 116, entered service in May 1955.

On 31 October, eighty-six trolleybuses (Nos 16–101) were licensed, the oldest being Nos 16–26, which were Leyland TB4s of 1937. The trolleybuses carried 41.8 million passengers (49 per cent of total passengers) and made a surplus of £28,386 (while motorbuses lost £33,300). The system was compact, comprising six routes with high-density frequencies, the busiest being service 70 at two minutes. As many workers went home for lunch, frequencies were increased between 12 noon and 2 p.m. The maximum fare was 4*d*, except on Sunday mornings, when it was 5*d*.

The remaining TB4s were steadily withdrawn until March 1955, the last being No. 25, along with un-rebuilt Crossley TDD4 No. 46. Eighty-nine trolleybuses were divided between four garages (not depots!). All the Leyland TB7s, Nos 47–66, were at Holderness Road, and the Crossleys and Coronations were at Cottingham Road, while Sunbeam Ws and F4s were shared between Liverpool Street and Wheeler Street. Eighty-three saw service on Saturday afternoons, and seventy-six during the week.

The operational hub was Queen Victoria Square, where all six routes could be observed. 8,853 journeys were made each week, with the most being 2,338 on service 70, and the least being 873 on service 61. If you had the time, every trolleybus in service could be seen.

Five routes terminated off the square (Hessle Road and Anlaby Road in Paragon Street and services 61/2/3 in King Edward Street). Services 64 and 68 passed through en route to Paragon Square. A green and white kiosk in King Edward Street housed the city centre inspector (for many years Stafford Rayner).

The busiest days were Fridays (after Thursday pay day) and Saturday. In addition to Saturday afternoon shoppers, trolleybuses carried fans to Hull City matches (service 69), Hull RLFC (service 71) and Hull Kingston Rovers (service 64). Vehicles would be borrowed from other garages for extra passengers (except for the Coronations), and the annual Hull Fair week in October generated substantial additional traffic. Walton Street was served at both ends by services 61 and 69, for which special timetables were operated. Inevitably, fairgoers mingled with ordinary traffic in the early evening and on Saturday.

Long queues formed at peak times at city centre termini, a result of the railway crossings that were present on each route. In Paragon Street, queues snaked around the corner into Chariot Street and Carr Lane. Passengers got wet and cold in winter while awaiting the appearance of what would often be three (or more) trolleybuses at a time. By 1955 there were still no shelters for passengers, who often used shop doorways to avoid the elements, leading to complaints from shopkeepers.

Coronation No. 116 received an electronic counting device on both stairs to assist the motorman in assessing how many seats were available in the upper deck. Its operation was inconsistent with No. 116 having to be changed over to effect repairs. It was removed when the manufacturer declined to continue with its development. No. 116 also received a Grant fare box, which was not used in service. The two-step entrance and exit proved unpopular and Mr Pulfrey promised that future deliveries would have flat platforms.

During the last decade, 155 repaints were carried out on the trolleybus fleet, the most being thirty-five in 1956/57, the least being just one in 1963. Each year some merely received a touch up and varnish, and there was no apparent decline in the standard of outward appearance. Between 1954 and 1960, thirty-three bodies received major overhauls. From 1954 flashing traffic indicators were fitted to all non-Coronation trolleybuses, the last being fitted in 1960.

The 1945 Brush-bodied Sunbeam Ws were subject to various degrees of rebuilding. All lost their upper front deck transom windows, while some received sliding windows in place of half-drop windows, and rubber radius curves were fitted to front upper deck windows and destination boxes. Nos 77 and 78 had the most alterations in the spring and summer of 1960.

In addition, the mid-1950s saw the end of the pre-war white blinds and wartime large number blinds, the last being (probably) No. 80.

The Coronations received additional centre door mirrors, a modified half bulkhead alongside the centre door and centre door warning lights. They also received modified sun visors. Their cabs were notoriously cold and many motormen wore bike clips to fasten their trousers to their socks, while some resorted to thermals or tights! All trolleybuses were fitted with suppressors to prevent interference with television reception.

Three shifts of three staff were each responsible for two routes of overhead line. One linesman considered the overhead lines to be in their best ever state by 1960. Tram traction poles from the former spur in Boothferry Road and Anlaby Road were used for roadworks at the Chanterlands Avenue South/Spring Bank West junction.

Two major re-routeing schemes were undertaken in the city centre. On 26 October 1958, service 70 was diverted from the narrow Midland Street and sent along Osborne Street and down Ferensway to rejoin the Anlaby Road overhead. In March 1959, the Holderness Road routes were diverted by a clockwise loop along Jameson Street, Chapel Street, Paragon Street, South Street and Jameson Street. The existing city centre loop was retained.

The Chanterlands Avenue route was the least remunerative and in November 1957 the frequency was altered so that the 65 to Goddard Avenue ran at off-peak times, thus reverting to the original service of 1937. Despite a rise in receipts per car mile, there was much criticism, and the 61 was restored on a reduced frequency. However, in its last years the 65 made a comeback.

In November 1957, three TB7s (50/60/62) were withdrawn to provide spares for the rest of the class. As patronage declined, there was an easing out of headways, although they remained intensive when compared with other systems.

In October 1958, a ten-year trolleybus renewal programme was approved by the Transport Committee. Mr Pulfrey proposed to buy ten 35-foot-long single-deck trolleybuses from Sunbeam for the Chanterlands Avenue route. After this, ten trolleybuses were to be purchased every two years. Some committee members called for a report about extending the system.

When this was presented it suggested abandonment of the system. Trolleybuses now carried 43 per cent of the total passengers and large housing clearance plans would relocate residents from trolleybus routes to areas far beyond the wires. A year-long debate ended with a City Council resolution in January 1960 to replace the trolleybuses.

Six more TB7s were withdrawn in August 1959 (47/9/51/3/7/8), being replaced by Crossleys transferred from Cottingham Road, which in turn acquired some 1947 Sunbeams that returned to their first garage. Further frequency reductions permitted another four TB7s (52/6/9/65) and Crossley No. 27 to be withdrawn in June 1960. This reduced the fleet to seventy-five (28–45/8/54/5/61/3/4/6–116). At various times TDD4s were working from Holderness Road alongside the remaining TB7s.

It was expected that the Hessle Road route, with its proximity to Liverpool Street Works, would be the last conversion, and one of the authors looked forward to sampling Coronations on a daily basis.

However, despite a turning circle being planned at the foot of a proposed road bridge at Dairycoates, it was decided to convert the 70 first. Therefore, on a Saturday in January 1961, all of the TB7s, as well as Crossleys Nos 28/9/33/6/44, were transferred to Liverpool Street, while several Sunbeam Ws went the other way. The TB7s and Crossleys were in place on Hessle Road but did not last long, closure coming on 28 January 1961. Leylands Nos 48/54/5/61/3/4/6 were in service on the final day, along with Crossleys Nos 29/33 and Sunbeams 71/4/81.

A wet and windy day saw the last trolleybuses during the evening, being (in order) 61/55/54/33/48. The last scheduled journey was worked by No. 48 from Paragon Street with a full load at 11 p.m. However, the last trolleybus was TDD4 No. 29, which left Liverpool Street for Paragon Street at 11.20 p.m. carrying at least one enthusiast to work a dance special. At 11.42 p.m. No. 29 departed with another full load of lively revellers, including one of the authors, reaching Dairycoates at 11.53 p.m. It returned to Liverpool Street, whose doors were then closed, ending sixty-two years of electric traction at the garage. Though the garage was closed operationally, it still saw trolleybuses for repair and after withdrawal, and it was not until March 1965 that the last Coronation left the building.

The Roe-bodied Sunbeams were concentrated at Wheeler Street while, according to official records, Nos 75–84 went to Holderness Road. However, ten vehicles would not have been sufficient to deliver a three-minute frequency and it appears that several of the 1947 Sunbeams were also working the service early in 1961, with Nos 70–74 at Cottingham Road and Nos 67–69 at Wheeler Street. Holderness Road had not been host to regular visits by Sunbeams so it was unusual to see them at work on the 64/8. Nos 91–100 had started life at Wheeler Street in June 1948, and so they were at home. However, a reallocation occurred in August 1961 when Nos 85–100 were sent to Holderness Road, which doesn't seem to have seen the F4s before. Nos 75–84 were sent to Wheeler Street to join 67-69.

The next casualty was Anlaby Road. To avoid problems with the delicate substation at Saner Street, the regenerative-equipped TDD4s were not transferred to Wheeler Street until the last possible moment. In mid-January the surviving Crossleys were transferred in exchange for the Sunbeam Ws. Saturday 3 February 1962 was the final day of operation, with No. 34 being the last service trolleybus from Paragon Street at 11 p.m. The redundant vehicles were towed to Liverpool Street the following day, with No. 39 being the last to leave.

They were joined at the end of February by Sunbeams Nos 67 and 68, with No. 67 skidding onto the pavement at Chanterlands Avenue South two days before withdrawal. Forty-eight trolleybuses were left: Nos 69-84/101–116 at Cottingham Road and Nos 85–100 at Holderness Road. Very unusually, in April 1962, F4 No. 92 was at Cottingham Road and worked on the 61/65 at least.

The arrival of RT buses from St Helens permitted the Chanterlands Avenue routes to be replaced in July 1962, the 65 succumbing on 27 July and the 61 on 28 July, twenty-five years after introduction. Coronation No. 105 worked the last journey at 11 p.m. Sunbeams Nos 69/71–4/9 were withdrawn and towed to Liverpool Street, but were not sold until May 1963. The overhead between Chanterlands Avenue North and Newland Avenue was retained for testing trolleybuses as final withdrawal was not expected until 1965.

A period of calm descended as trolleybuses were repaired and repainted while driver training continued. Plenty of trolleybuses could still be seen at the Jameson Street/King Edward Street junction.

September 1963 saw another round of transfers take place, with Nos 91–100 going to Cottingham Road and 70/5–8/80–4 going to Holderness Road. No. 90 worked the last journey on the 64 at 11 p.m. on Saturday 21 September.

In anticipation of another year's service, F4s Nos 97 and 100 received repaints. Their time was cut short, however, as there were surplus buses with the completion of extensive repairs to the Regent III fleet, and it was decided that the Newland Avenue route would be replaced. F4 No. 94 performed the last sombre journey on 16 November 1963 at 11 p.m. As Liverpool Street was full of withdrawn trolleybuses and diesels, they were stored for a time at the back of Holderness Road Garage.

All sixteen Coronations were retained for the Beverley Road route. A new one-way system in the city centre was introduced on 28 June 1964, which saw the 63 diverted along Paragon Street, Chapel Street and Jameson Street. However, a few months later, on a very damp and misty Saturday 31 October, No. 101, without ceremony and preceded by No. 116, worked the last journey from Chapel Street at 11 p.m., ending sixty-five years of electric traction in the city of Hull. Despite a tender submitted by the Reading Transport Society, no Coronation was saved for posterity. In their time, some 887,387,582 passengers were carried and 55,839,158 miles were run, with some £474,000 profit accumulated.

At the beginning of 1954, twenty-one Leyland TB4s of 1937 were still in service. In March, No. 17 was working from Liverpool Street garage and is seen here with Sunbeam F4 No. 92. (LS)

In April 1954, No. 13 is shown turning across the reservation at Meadowbank Road terminus of route 69, complete with wartime large route number blind above the platform. (LS)/(RFM)

Also in April, No. 23 was resting quietly at the Newland Avenue terminus of route 62. The photograph shows the simple, clear lines of the seventeen-year-old Weymann body to good effect. (LS)/(RFM)

This is the inward stop at Dairycoates, with Sunbeam W No. 74 and an F4 behind. It must be cold as the motorman (driver, in Hull parlance) is wearing his winter overcoat. It's possible that No. 74 has not yet received its cab heater. (LS)/(RFM)

A trio of Leyland TB7s seen in Holderness Road garage yard before the direction of travel was reversed for the installation of a bus washing machine. Note the white lines to guide trolleybuses. (LS)

The U-turn at the Newland Avenue/Cottingham Road terminus was not easy, as demonstrated by No. 21 in May 1954. (LS)

When one of the four railway crossings that crossed a trolleybus route was closed for repairs (usually on Sunday mornings), it was practice to run trolleybuses to both sides of the crossing and transfer passengers over the crossing. Trolleybuses turned by reversing into a side street to the maximum extent of the booms, as demonstrated by Crossley No. 39 on Beverley Road. (LS)

Brush-bodied Sunbeam W No. 74 has just arrived at the outward stop at Meadowbank Road. (LS)/(RFM)

Another photograph at Meadowbank Road with Sunbeam F4 No. 97 overtaking two Crossleys, which are awaiting the final whistle at Hull City's Boothferry Park ground, which is just around the corner. Trolleybuses were borrowed from other garages on match days and usually laid over in Wheeler Street garage nearby. (LS)/(RFM)

Leyland TB4 No. 21 waits patiently for passengers at the Chanterlands Avenue North terminus of route 61 in June 1954. As usual, there is little business at this location. (LS)

Another view of No. 21 as it passes the turning circle for route 66 at Pearson Park on Princes Avenue in June 1954. (LS)

In the same month, Crossley TDD4 No. 33 makes its way along a deserted Beverley Road. Twenty Crossleys with Cravens H54R bodywork (later H60R) opened this route in September 1938. (LS)/(RFM)

A full Leyland TB4 pulls away from the stop opposite the Northern Branch Library on Beverley Road, bound for Endike Lane on 19 June 1954. It also has a pre-war blind over the platform. (AC)

The road under the Hull & Barnsley Railway bridge on Chanterlands Avenue was prone to flood in wet weather, but on this dry July day Leyland TB4 No. 26 has no such problems en route to King Edward Street. (LS)/(RFM)

Sunbeam W No. 87 with Roe H60R bodywork loads at the 70 barrier in Paragon Street. When new, all six Sunbeams had been allocated to Cottingham Road. (AC)

Three trolleybuses with three different bodywork designs at Dairycoates. No. 93 occupies the turning circle and one of its traction poles appears to be leaning over. Alongside the circle is a police box, which is soon to be removed. (LS)/(RFM)

As 1954 wore on the bodywork repairs to the Cravens-bodied Crossleys were completed and the Coronations began to arrive. The result was the steady withdrawal of the TB4s, and a withdrawn No. 11 languishes in Liverpool Street in November. (LS)

A sunny day in December at an unusually quiet Dairycoates terminus. The Brush-bodied Sunbeam Ws had opened the route on 1 July 1945 in an all-blue livery. The bodywork is as delivered, although seating has been increased to sixty. (LS)/(RFM)

A welcome sight for any trolleybus enthusiast. Newly delivered Sunbeam MF2B No. 110 with Roe H54D bodywork stands in Liverpool Street in December. It will enter service on New Year's Day in 1955. On the left is the duty board, which shows Nos 24/70/68/20 as 'Stopped' and Nos 72 and 91 as spare. (LS)

Sunbeam W No. 80 carried a 'relaxed' Roe utility body when delivered in late 1945. Here it is turning at Meadowbank Road in February 1955. It has a white blind, which shows the original 'Wheeler Street' destination used before the extension to Meadowbank Road in March 1947. (LS)/(RFM)

The conductor has changed the blind to indicate that it will return to 'CITY', which was used rather than a street name, despite the fact that everyone said they were going to 'town'. It has yet to receive the final version of the 'Corporation Transport' rectangle. (LS)/(RFM)

Sunbeam Ws Nos 68 and 87 rest at Dairycoates. No. 68 has lost the front upper deck transom windows in the first of many alterations to the twelve-strong class over the next five years. (LS)/(RFM)

Both the Anlaby Road and Hessle Road routes terminated in Carr Lane, outside the City Hall, before turning across the front of the Hall into Paragon Street to reach their respective stands. No. 71 is followed by No. 93. Note the wall plate for the overhead wires. (LS)/(RFM)

No. 116 was the last Coronation to enter service in May 1955. It carried an experimental windscreen, which was soon replaced. No. 116 is on trade plates at Newland Avenue during testing by the Engineers Department when seen. (LS)

A view inside the paint shop in Liverpool Street, with Leyland TB7 No. 58 almost ready to return to service (usually on Friday lunchtime). It was one of twenty-two trolleybuses repainted in 1955/56. (LS)

Sunbeam W No. 82 draws away from a stop on Hessle Road near Westbourne Street, which Malcolm used regularly. It is travelling to the city centre in July 1955. (LS)/(RFM)

No. 83 is seen here turning at Dairycoates as another trolleybus leaves for Paragon Street. (LS)/(RFM)

Six-month-old Coronation No. 110 has vacated Cottingham Road garage and has taken the nearside wires to enable it to turn left into Beverley Road and travel to the Endike Lane terminus. (LS)

The time is 7.30 p.m. on Monday 24 October 1955, with three trolleybuses at their respective stands in King Edward Street. Note the well-lit interior of No. 111 and that all trolleybuses are using side lights, as was standard in those days. (LS)

A well-lit and (hopefully) warm Sunbeam W No. 70 in Paragon Street, an experience which Malcolm had every night, travelling home from school. All of Hull's trolleybuses had saloon heating from the beginning in 1937. The remnants of the original passenger shelter are still in situ (but not for long!). (LS)

It was rare for a Leyland TB7 to stray from Holderness Road, but in February 1956 No. 56 found itself working on the 70 to Dairycoates at Porter Street, a stop that was well-used at peak times. (LS)/(RFM)

Although all ten Sunbeam F4s were allocated to Wheeler Street when new in June 1948, by 1956 they were evenly divided between there and Liverpool Street. No. 91 is at the 70 barrier in Paragon Street as its crew chats through the open nearside door. (LS)/(RFM)

Sunbeam W No. 90 rests in the winter sun at Dairycoates before moving up the stop. (AC)

Crossley TDD4 No. 28 waits while a school party disembarks on Chanterlands Avenue near Goddard Avenue. As this is June, it could be a working in connection with the Northern Hull School's Sports Day at Oak Road Playing Fields, which adjoined the Endike Lane (63) terminus. (LS)/(RFM)

A typical quiet Chanterlands Avenue North terminus with Crossley TDD4 No. 28 at rest. The white line on the fence, which was supposed to assist drivers with placing trolleybuses so as not to block drives, can be seen. (LS)/(RFM)

On 3 December 1956, No. 40 has just arrived in King Edward Street from Newland Avenue and will shortly work around the statue in Queen Victoria Square to reach the vacant 62 stand. Note the inspector (possibly Stafford Rayner) in his little hut adjoining the 61 stand. (LS)

In 1956 a new bus washer was installed in Holderness Road garage, which necessitated the direction of travel for trolleybuses and diesels to be reversed. Leyland TB7 No. 48 leaves the washer to proceed to the garage building. (LS)

Until the last days of the Hessle Road route, Malcolm never saw a Crossley on the 70, so it was a surprise to find this photograph of No. 42 in Paragon Street. (LS)/(RFM)

Sunbeam F4 No. 96, having unloaded its remaining passengers, will proceed around the City Hall into Paragon Street. (LS)/(RFM)

No. 88 has just reversed at Malm Street after working a rugby league special for Hull RLFC. It appears to be losing its trolley booms. It was unusual to display 69 rather than 71 on these workings. (LS)/(RFM)

King Edward Street, which housed the termini for routes 61/2/3/5/6, was very busy in this August 1957 view. At peak times fifty-three trolleybus workings were scheduled to terminate here. (LS)/(RFM)

Another rare sight was Leyland TB7 No. 49 turning into Cottingham Road from Beverley Road, possibly working a school sports special from East Hull. (LS)

Saturday 11 October 1957 was another busy day in King Edward Street, with the normal shopper traffic boosted by people going to the yearly Hull Fair (the largest in the UK). Crossley No. 27 overtakes Coronation No. 110. Note the 'TO THE FAIR' sticker in the nearside windscreen of No. 31. (LS)/(RFM)

No. 88 turns across the reservation at Meadowbank Road, a location which was a favourite position for photographers. (AC)

No. 88 again, this time at Paragon Street, where it has not yet moved on to the stand. The shelters have gone, being replaced with a barrier and a very clear and informative stop sign. (LS)/(RFM)

It's Polling Day and the conductor of Crossley No. 30 looks on as it turns to reach the inward stop at Chanterlands Avenue North. (LS)/(RFM)

A quiet nocturnal view in Paragon Street in February 1958 as No. 89 departs the 69 stand before overtaking No. 83 on the 70 stand. (LS)

Hull City and Hull RLFC matches generated many special workings along Anlaby Road, with vehicles being borrowed from other garages to cope with the extra numbers. Cottingham Road resident No. 43 has just offloaded its supporters and will take the left-hand wires into the Boulevard to reverse at Malm Street. The trolleybus stop plate, coloured green, can be seen. (LS)/(RFM)

Leyland TB7 No. 47 is in Ferensway on its way to the setting down stop outside the Station Hotel in October 1958. It will then cross the square to reach the terminus outside the Hammonds department store. (LS)/(RFM)

October 1958 also saw another TB7 on a rugby special duty as No. 52 leaves the Boulevard to return to Paragon Street. (LS)/(RFM)

The interior of the trolleybus shed at Holderness Road was compact and could hold twenty-one vehicles, although twenty was the normal allocation. Nos 55 and 66 head the group in October 1958. (LS)

Also in October 1958, No. 64 is dwarfed by the Hull Savings Bank head office as it turns into Savile Street from George Street. (LS)/(RFM)

Sunday 28 October 1958 was the first day's use of the new route 70 inward overhead along Osborne Street and the new section of Ferensway. F4 No. 95 is turning from Ferensway into Anlaby Road. (LS)

Leyland TB7 No. 47 inches cautiously past the overhead linesmen near Anne Street. When the 64 is diverted in March 1959, the through wires will be changed to Anlaby Road. (LS)/(RFM)

As part of the preparations for that diversion, a temporary siding was installed outside the existing terminus at Hammonds. Not all trolleybus drivers used this, as evidenced here on 26 October 1958. (LS)/(RFM)

The East Lancashire bodywork is illustrated here as No. 66 turns at Ings Road. The nearside cab door would have been standard had the war not intervened. (LS)/(RFM)

Leyland TB7 No. 56, newly fitted with a flashing traffic indicator, stands at the original terminus outside Hammonds. The Hammonds canopy provided some protection for waiting passengers. (LS)/(RFM)

By February 1959 three TB7s had been withdrawn and Crossley No. 45 had been sent to Holderness Road garage as a replacement. On 8 February 1959, No. 45 was used to test the new overhead, and is seen here in Paragon Street under newly erected wires. (LS)

Also in February, No. 57 passes Sunbeam No. 79 in Carr Lane. No. 79 has had its disused rear destination box removed and No. 57 would be withdrawn in August. (LS)/(RFM)

The maximum permitted speed along Spring Bank West was 25 mph. On a Sunday morning this was nearly always attained with, in later years, many noisy body rattles. No. 31 is probably trying its best to achieve the 25 mph. (LS)/(RFM)

On Sunday mornings it was possible to ride on Crossleys on the 63, allegedly to maintain drivers' familiarity with them – or, according to others, because Les Storry decreed it! On 5 July 1959, Crossleys reign supreme in King Edward Street! (LS)/(RFM)

Another Sunday in July, with No. 40 accompanied by Coronations. (LS)/(RFM)

No. 40 again on another sunny Sunday in July, about to turn into Spring Bank from Princes Avenue. The white circle on the road was the location of the police traffic control box at peak times! (LS)/(RFM)

Crossley No. 41 accelerates away from Chanterlands North as a Coronation eases on to the stand. (LS)/(RFM)

Also at Chanterlands Avenue North, Coronation No. 106 leaves the terminus and has negotiated the frog at the southern end of the central reservation. (LS)/(RFM)

Following the withdrawal of six TB7s in August 1959, several Crossleys were moved to Holderness Road, although it seems that they may have been rotated. No. 34 has just left the garage and is turning towards Ings Road. (AC)

No. 34 is seen again at the Ings Road terminus. (LS)/(RFM)

TDD4 No. 28 is at rest at Newland Avenue and wears its twenty-one years well, despite a trademark cab door, which has slipped. (VN)

TB7 No. 48 was one of the survivors in 1959 and looks in good form outside the Imperial Hotel under the new overhead in Paragon Street. (LS)/(RFM)

On 30 July, Coronation No. 109 is on tuition duty at the southern end of the reservation in Chanterlands Avenue North. This turning circle was once used by wartime service 67 (ex-63A) and is now used for test runs from Cottingham Road garage. (LS)

Coronation No. 103 has made the short journey from Cottingham Road garage and its conductor is about to operate the frog to allow it to turn into Newland Avenue. (LS)/(RFM)

Both entrances into Cottingham Road garage required conductors to operate frogs, in order to cut down excessive speeds and avoid dewirements, according to management. Beverley Road-bound trolleybuses also needed the conductor to operate the chain. (LS)

Crossley TDD4 No. 30 passes the former Thornton Varley department store (complete with wall plates), just two stops away from King Edward Street. (LS)/(RFM)

Trolleybuses pass at Goddard Avenue in September 1959. Crossley No. 33 is city-bound while Coronation No. 101 is at the stop opposite. It is running without retrievers (not a rare event with No. 101). The red triangle is a bit superfluous. (LS)/(RFM)

Coronation No. 108 is about to turn right from Cottingham Road into Beverley Road to travel to King Edward Street. Normally, trolleybuses took up service from Endike Lane, so this is a rare shot! (LS)

Crossley TDD4 No. 33 has just come from Cottingham Road garage and will turn from Cottingham Road into Chanterlands Avenue North. It was possible to ride between the garage and Chanterlands Avenue (2*d* for adults, 1*d* for children). (LS)/(RFM)

We see No. 33 again, turning into Spring Bank West from Chanterlands Avenue. Also in view are the overhead fog lights and the tied-back overhead, erected in connection with roadworks at this junction. (LS)/(RFM)

Coronation No. 103 makes the turn at the same junction with a clearer view of the second set of overhead erected for the new line to be taken after road works. (LS)/(RFM)

A quiet Sunday at this normally busy junction with Coronation No. 102 about to turn into Princes Avenue. The wires on the right lead into Spring Bank West. (LS)/(RFM)

One of the dwindling numbers of Leyland TB7s, No. 54, is seen in Jameson Street amid Christmas lights, en route for Paragon Street. (LS)/(RFM)

Crossley No. 43 is ready to leave Cottingham Road garage on learner duties, while Coronation No. 103 awaits entry. Driver training continued until 11 August 1964. (LS)/(RFM)

In addition to Crossleys transferred to Holderness Road, Sunbeam W No. 85 was working on the 64/8 in May 1960 as four more Leyland TB7s succumbed. This view was taken from the stairway inside the Hammonds department store. (LS)/(RFM)

A fine side view of Coronation No. 110 at Chanterlands Avenue North, also in May 1960, with foreman fitter and photographer Les Storry at the wheel! (LS)/(RFM)

Views of TB7s in South Street are rare. This one of No. 48 was taken by Malcolm in June 1960, a month which saw another four TB7s taken out of service. (MJW)

Sunbeam F4 No. 98 is leaving Wheeler Street garage but is turning towards 'town' rather than towards Meadowbank Road. (LS)/(RFM)

A very rainy June day sees Sunbeam F4 No. 100 passing the Boulevard, about to negotiate the level crossing en route to Meadowbank Road. (LS)/(RFM)

A Crossley on a rugby special duty, No. 38 is about to leave the Boulevard to return to Paragon Street. (LS)/(RFM)

A sylvan scene in August taken from Pearson Park on Princes Avenue with No. 40 inward bound. (LS)/(RFM)

By now No. 48 is one of only seven remaining TB7s, and has less than six months' service left. It is leaving North Bridge. (LS)/(RFM)

As TB7s were withdrawn there was general (and flexible) shuffling of trolleybuses between garages. Sunbeam No. 84 is now working from Cottingham Road. It leads Coronation No. 110 into Queen Victoria Square. Across the road No. 40 is parked up, waiting for its trolley heads to be repaired. (LS)/(RFM)

The overhead line gang have arrived to treat No. 40, while Coronation No. 106, having disgorged its passengers, is about turn round the square. The overhead wires to the right lead into Savile Street and formed the original route 64 terminal loop. (LS)/(RFM)

Another rainy day on the 69. Sunbeam W No. 81 shivers in the rain at Meadowbank Road. (LS)/(RFM)

Despite withdrawal not being far away, Leyland TB7 No. 54 has received a repaint complete with white hand rails on the upper deck front windows. The location is Ings Road. (LS)/(RFM)

Crossley No. 35 was one of several TDD4s that worked from Holderness Road to replace withdrawn TB7s. It rests at the terminus near the *Daily Mail* office in Jameson Street. (JF)

Les Storry is pictured at work inside Cottingham Road garage during August 1960 on Coronation No. 103 while Crossley No. 36 looks on. (LS)/(RFM)

Coronations Nos 105 and 111 are at the 63 barrier in King Edward Street, with not a service 61 or 62 in sight. (LS)

A newly repainted trolleybus was always welcome and No. 76 shows off its new coat in Anne Street on 20 June 1960. (LS)

There is little room to manoeuvre as Crossley No. 41, having worked a Hull Fair special in October 1960, turns at Chanterlands Avenue South. Operations were supervised by an inspector. (LS)/(RFM)

Crossleys pass near Pearson Park in December 1960. No. 41 is working a Christmas extra on the 66 while No. 28, which has less than two months of work left, is on the 62. Motorman Pat Kerrins is stood on the right and later drove the final service 62 on 16 November 1963. (LS)/(RFM)

A late evening scene in Cottingham Road garage in December. The two Coronations may be about to work dance specials, or Les Storry might have played with the destination numbers! (LS)

On the first Saturday in 1961, the remaining Leyland TB7s and five Crossleys were transferred to Liverpool Street in anticipation of the 70 conversion. No. 28 is at Dairycoates during the last week of operation. (AC)

The TB7s looked out of place with the 70 in the destination box, but they soldiered on in the last weeks. No. 48 is in Chariot Street on Saturday 28 January 1961, the final day of the service. (LS)

Another view of No. 48 as it enters Paragon Street on the final day of trolleybus operation on service 70, Saturday 28 January 1961, while a Crossley heads for the 61 stand in King Edward Street. (AC)

Sunbeams Nos 69–74 and 81 were retained at Liverpool Street until the last day of service 70. No. 81 was transferred to Cottingham Road on that day, while No. 48 will be withdrawn and remain in the then closed Liverpool Street. (AC)

Crossley TDD4 No. 43 is working an extra run on the 66 for Easter and is seen here entering Spring Bank. (LS)/(RFM)

After the closure of the Hessle Road route, the F4s were concentrated at Wheeler Street for a time before going to Holderness Road in August. In March, No. 93 is approaching the entrance to the garage and ignores Mrs Arbela Johnson, who is on her hands and knees washing the steps of her home! (LS)

There were sixty-two trolleybuses still in service and the section between Blundells Corner and King Edward Street enjoyed forty-four trolleybus journeys at the evening peak. Several can be seen opposite Hull Royal Infirmary. (LS)/(RFM)

What looks like a repainted Coronation No. 102 awaits departure time (and passengers!) at Goddard Avenue during April 1961. (LS)

In May 1961, after receiving a repaint, another Coronation, No. 103, is to be towed to Cottingham Road garage. This was normal practice even when Hessle Road was still wired. (LS)

Having completed its turn of duty, No. 112 has left Endike Lane and is preparing to turn into Cottingham Road to reach the garage during May 1961. (LS)/(RFM)

Having escaped the route 70 cull, Crossley No. 42 remained active and is seen accelerating away from the Chanterlands Avenue/Bricknell Avenue roundabout. (LS)

On 19 April 1961, Sunbeam W No. 82 stands quietly at Ings Road. (DT)

Some of the 1947 Sunbeams were transferred to Cottingham Road. Their work seems not to have attracted the photographers but No. 88 was at Goddard Avenue in May. (LS)/(RFM)

Crossley No. 41 has Chanterlands Avenue North to itself as it passes Allderidge Avenue in July 1961. (LS)/(RFM)

Brush-bodied Sunbeam W No. 77 eases away from the Hull & Barnsley Railway bridge on Newland Avenue. (JS)

The rear of Sunbeam W No. 84 reveals that the rear destination box has been painted over. The location is Pearson Park. (JS)

With yet another Hull & Barnsley Railway bridge in the background, Sunbeam W No. 70 is at the Meadowbank Road terminus. (LS)/(RFM)

A well-filled Crossley No. 32 passes gently over the Botanic Gardens railway crossing en route to Goddard Avenue on 25 August 1961. (LS)/(RFM)

No. 38 has just three months left in service when seen at a stop often used by Malcolm after visiting his grandmother. The moped is Les Storry's and is often seen in trolleybus pictures around the city. (LS)

Two Crossleys meet on Chanterlands Avenue near Newstead Street in October 1961. No. 32 is nearest the camera, while No. 35, complete with painted over rear destination box, stands on the left. (LS)/(RFM)

Sunbeam W No. 77 stands outside Robinson's shop in South Street on 26 November 1961. Its Brush body had seen modified front upper windows, sliding vents and rubber mounts around the destination box. (MJW)

Sunbeam No. 74 collects a solitary passenger at Botanic Gardens on a pre-Christmas 66 working. Les Storry's well-pictured moped can be seen again! (LS)

Another pre-Christmas extra, though this time worked by Coronation No. 106 on Spring Bank. (LS)/(RFM)

With the transfer of the Crossleys to Wheeler Street, the end for the 69 is approaching. No. 41 waits at Meadowbank Road in January 1962. (LS)/(RFM)

The Crossleys were assisted by some Sunbeam Ws, such as No. 69, which is about to leave the narrow exit at Wheeler Street, a relic of tramway days. No. 69 was the only Brush-bodied version to have the white line run above the destination box. (LS)

Standing outside the narrow exit road of the Wheeler Street depot we see the crew, including Motorman Ron Green with the white cap, on the left, and three inspectors on the right, posing for Les Storry with Crossley No. 32 on the final day of trolleybus operation on the Anlaby Road service. (AC)

On the final day again we see Crossley No. 30 heading back into 'town', having just crossed the Newington level crossing on Anlaby Road. The following day would see brand-new Leyland Atlanteans take over operations. (MJW)

Also on 3 February, several Crossley trolleybuses await their entry into service at Wheeler Street. (MB)

Crossley No. 34 awaits passengers before making the last journey to Meadowbank Road. (MB)

A sad sight on the following day was the transfer of each trolleybus to Liverpool Street under tow by the department's wagon. This is No. 38. (LS)

Just three days from a road accident that led to its withdrawal, Sunbeam W No. 67 pulls away from the kiosk outside Hull Royal Infirmary on 20 February. (AC)

Sunbeam W No. 76 leads No. 86 along Holderness Road towards Ings Road. (JF)

In March 1962, No. 71 crosses Blundell's Corner on a 65 working to King Edward Street. (LS)/(RFM)

Sunbeam W No. 86 stands at the stop outside the *Hull Daily Mail* offices. The former wires across Paragon Square have been removed after the 69 conversion. (LS)/(RFM)

In March and April, Sunbeam F4 No. 92 worked from Cottingham Road – the only instance of such a working to that date. It is seen here at the Chanterlands Avenue/Bricknell Avenue roundabout. Note the post-war prefab homes behind. (LS)/(RFM)

On 11 March, the crew and inspector enjoy a chat while F4 No. 96 stands quietly at the Jameson Street terminus. (AC)

A quiet night-time view of Coronation No. 116 at Goddard Avenue. (AC)

Two fine examples of Roe bodywork meet at Goddard Avenue in April 1962. F4 No. 92 passes Coronation No. 107. (LS)/(RFM)

Roe-bodied Sunbeam W No. 86 basks in the Sunday sunshine on 17 June at Newland Avenue. (MJW)

Sunbeam No. 74 is about to pass into Spring Bank from Spring Bank West, en route to King Edward Street. (JS)

Coronation No. 111 turns into Prospect Street at Blundells Corner. In the distance is a Sunbeam W also on the 63, which was not usual on weekdays. (JS)

Sunbeam No. 70 prepares to leave Goddard Avenue in March 1962. (LS)

With just a few days of service left, Sunbeam W No. 73, with Motorman Norman Brannon at the wheel, leads Coronation No. 102 along Chanterlands Avenue. (LS)/(RFM)

The last ever route 65 journey to King Edward Street from Goddard Avenue was worked by Roe-bodied Sunbeam W No. 81 on Friday 27 July 1962. (LS)

Three trolleybuses on three different routes travel towards the city centre in Prospect Street at the Story Street junction. Sunbeam W No. 82 leads the trio. Note the overhead wires attached to the rosettes on the wall. (LS)/(RFM)

A lightly loaded No. 74 nears the Chanterlands Avenue North terminus in the last days of the 61/65 trolleybus service during July 1962. Les Storry's moped is again seen in the view! (LS)

Sunbeam No. 77 is seen at rest on the last day of the 61 at Chanterlands Avenue. (MJW)

Coronation No. 105 is about to depart from King Edward Street to work the last 61 journey at 11 p.m. on 28 July 1962, with Motorman Jim Marshall and Conductor Bill Fielding. (LS)

In July 1962, Sunbeam W No. 82 is seen passing Cottingham Road while on driver tuition duties. Driver (motorman) training continued until August 1964. (LS)/(RFM)

In August 1961, the F4s were concentrated at Holderness Road, along with the 1947 Sunbeams. Malcolm's own favourite, No. 95, passes a sister F4 on Holderness Road near Southcoates railway station. (LS)/(RFM)

This view shows how essential the piece cut out of the pavement was to facilitate the U-turn at Newland Avenue/Cottingham Road. Had the City Engineer had his own way in 1937 this manoeuvre would have been banned. (PC)

This shows No. 78, whose Brush body received (in May 1960) the full treatment with sliding windows, no transom and rubber mounted/radiussed destination box and upper deck windows. (AC)

This rear view of No. 84 shows the painted over rear destination box. (AC)

Sunbeams Nos 86 and 93 stand in the pale sunshine at Ings Road in October 1962. (PC)

Also in October, Sunbeam W No. 82 is about to turn at Newland Avenue. (PC)

At East Park the conductor prepares to operate the frog to enable No. 90 to cross the reservation and return to 'town' in April 1963. (LS)/(RFM)

Sunbeam F4 No. 97 threads its way through a busy Chapel Street on its way to the terminus in Paragon Street. (LS)/(RFM)

A turning facility was erected at Malton Street in 1956/7 in anticipation of major work at North Bridge. Passengers would transfer to a diesel to reach and come from Jameson Street. It was also used by school sports specials to East Park. No. 98 approaches Malton Street from North Bridge. (TB)

Coronation No. 113 turns across Queen Victoria Square to reach King Edward Street. Garage journeys on the 63 usually worked to and from Endike Lane. (JS)

In July two Sunbeams meet at East Park, with No. 89 approaching the turnaround junction. (AC)

This view gives a close picture of the bridgework of North Bridge. The trolleybus is No. 90. (JS)

Conductor and motorman exchange views through the open nearside door at Ings Road. (AC)

Sunbeam No. 88 leads two F4s towards Summergangs Road. The camber here was the subject of many complaints by motormen and was prone to dewirements. (JS)

On Saturday 21 September 1963, the last day of the Holderness Road trolleybuses, Sunbeam W No. 81 passes East Park en route back into 'town'. (LS)/(RFM)

Also on the last day, Sunbeam W No. 89 has already collected several passengers as it passes Holderness Road garage. (LS)/(RFM)

Motorman Charles Karis eases the last Holderness Road trolleybus across North Bridge towards Ings Road just after 11 p.m. on Saturday 21 September 1963. This photograph gives us a good view of the cab switches. (LS)

Enthusiasts looked forward to another year of the Sunbeam F4s, as it seemed did the Transport Department. A newly repainted No. 100 is on a test run on Beverley Road on 17 October 1963. (LS)

On 25 September, No. 96 shows off its impressive Charles H. Roe front at Newland Avenue. (MJW)

Sadly, the Sunbeam F4s' reign on Newland Avenue was cut short, and on Saturday 16 November the route was withdrawn. F4s Nos 91 and 100 contemplate their fate at the Newland Avenue terminus during the final afternoon. (LS)

Just the 63 remained as Coronation No. 104 nears Harley Street on Beverley Road, bound for King Edward Street. (LS)/(RFM)

No. 113 was the first trolleybus to use the new overhead line, which was necessitated by the introduction of a one-way system in the city centre. The date is Sunday 28 June 1964, just after lunchtime, and all eyes are on this motorman as he makes that first turn! (JS)

The new left turn into King Edward Street from Jameson Street was very tight and an unidentified Coronation takes the junction cautiously, also on 28 June 1964. (JS)

Workmen were still painting the road markings on the first day as No. 111 passes the inspector's kiosk. (JS)

The new 63 terminus was in Chapel Street, where No. 102 has just arrived on 22 August 1964. (AC)

Coronation No. 115 drops passengers off at the new setting-down point in Paragon Street. (MJW)

No. 116, which would work the penultimate journey from Chapel Street, passes local landmark the Haworth (Hayworth in Hull speak) Arms at the Cottingham Road junction on 31 October, the last day. (JS)

No. 107 was among the last Coronations at work on the last evening, and is seen in Chapel Street, waiting time. (AC)

The last ever trolleybus journey (with Malcolm aboard) was worked by prototype Coronation No. 101, crewed by Gill Sewell and John Leonard. With no official acknowledgement of the event, it left Chapel Street at 11 p.m. on Saturday 31 October 1964. On arrival at Endike Lane, it took much persuasion for an inspector to allow enthusiasts to ride back to Cottingham Road. (LS)

Acknowledgements

The majority of photographs seen in this book were taken by the late Les Storry, who was the foreman fitter based at Cottingham Road Depot. His passion for the Hull system can be clearly seen in his views, as can quite often his little moped or push bike. He gave several photographs to Malcolm when he was researching for his history published by Trolleybooks (1996). He was very good friends with the late Bob Mack and passed many of his negatives to him over the years. Bob himself was also a well-known UK trolleybus photographer. Thanks also go to Bob Rowe at Trolleybooks for images, and we also have pictures from John Simpson, John Fozzard and Mike Baxter.

Where we know who the photographer is, each picture carries their initials, but many are not known so all credit must go to the wonderful people who took the time to come to Hull to capture the trolleybus fleet in action. These are marked with (AC). Our combined collections have been built over the past thirty to fifty years, so sadly it is not always possible to put a name to a print; apologies to anyone we may have missed.